Published by
Enete Enterprises

6504 N Omaha Ave
Oklahoma City, OK 73116 (USA)

1ˢᵗ publication of
Becoming an Expat COOKBOOK: Costa Rica

Copyright © Enete Enterprises, LLC; 2014
All rights reserved

*** Becoming an Expat Guidebook Series ***

Schmidt, Mike & Joellyn

Becoming an Expat COOKBOOK: Costa Rica / Mike & Joellyn Schmidt

ISBN-13: 978-1938216060
ISBN-10: 1938216067

Printed in the United States of America
www.EneteEnterprises.com

The scanning, uploading, and distribution of this book via the internet or any other means without the permission of Enete Enterprises, LLC is illegal. Please do not participate in electronic piracy of copyrightable materials.

OTHER BOOKS BY

BECOMING AN EXPAT

Becoming an Expat: **Costa Rica**
Becoming an Expat: **Ecuador**
Becoming an Expat: **Thailand**

UPCOMING BOOKS

Becoming an Expat 101
Becoming an Expat: **Brazil**
Becoming an Expat: **Mexico**
Becoming a **Nomad**

visit: www.Becominganexpat.com

✦to see updates in-between editions
✦for additional resources
✦to discover what we come up with next!

DEDICATION

This Cookbook is dedicated to the ladies that started our culinary training: Frances Raylene Overstreet (Jo's Mom), Virginia Mary Schmidt (Mike's Mom), Mary Jimetta Anderson (Jo's Aunt), and Virginia Overstreet (Jo's Grandma).

TABLE OF CONTENTS

Costa Rican Cuisine 101..................................... 11
    Staple Foods.. 12
    Sock Coffee... 13
    Eggs... 14
    Produce.. 14

Picking Produce 101.. 17
Food Hacks.. 25
Basic Metric Conversions................................ 27

Seasonings, Marinades & Dressings.................. 31
    Taco Seasoning....................................... 33
    Blacking Spice... 34
    Chili Powder.. 35
    Citrus Mojo Marinade.............................. 36
    Costa Rican Marinade............................. 37
    Ranch Dressing....................................... 38

Batidos (Smoothies) & Refrescos..................... 39
    Basic Batido/Smoothie Recipe................ 41
    Fresh Mango/Banana Batido.................. 42
    Fresh Strawberry/Banana Batido........... 43
    Fresh Pineapple/Coconut Batido............ 44
    Guanabana Batido.................................. 45
    Tamarind Refresco.................................. 46

Salas, Guacamole, & Appetizers..................... 47
    Olive Oil Dipping Sauce.......................... 49
    Fresh Mango & Peach Salsa.................. 50
    Guacamole.. 51
    Guacamole with Feta Cheese................ 53
    Pico de Gallo.. 54
    Stuffed Avocados................................... 55
    Queso Fritto... 56

Main Dishes... 57
Chicken (Pollo).. 59
    Chicken (pollo) en salsa......................... 61

Rosemary Chicken	62
Fried Chicken	63

Seafood **65**
Seared Tuna Steaks with Ginger-Lime Sauce	67
Baked Tilapia	68
Blackened Corvina	69
Shrimp Etouffee	70

Beef **73**
Jojo's Meatloaf	75
Shepherd's Pie	77
Breaded Bistec (steak)	79
Sloppy Joe's	80
Ameri-Rican Stew	81
Jojo's Spaghetti with Albendingas (meatballs)	83

Pork **85**
Stuffed Pork Sirloin Tip Roast	87
Mojo Marinated Pork Chops	89
Pulled Pork Sliders	90
Chicharrón Cerdo	91

Vegetarian **93**
Thai Stir-fry	95
No Crust Feta & Kale Quiche	97
Vegetarian Lasagna	98
Eggplant Parmesan	99
Stuffed Chayote	100

Soup **101**
Chili Con Carne with Beans	103
Garbanzo Bean Soup	104
Vegetable Beef Soup	105
Quick Chicken Noodle Soup	106

Salads **107**
Cucumber/Orange/Tomato Salad	109
Cobb Salad	110
Tomato Caprese	111
Kale and Tomato Salad with Blue Cheese	112

Potatoes, Rice, Pasta, & Yucca **113**
    Mojo Yucca 115
    Yucca Hash 116
    Potato Salad 118
    French Fries & Yucca Fries 119
    Costa Rican Rice 120
    Gallo Pinto 121

Vegetables **123**
    Roasted Cauliflower with Lime Sauce 125
    Roasted Broccoli with Balsamic Vinegar 127
    Coleslaw 128
    Caramelized Carrots 129
    Wilted Kale and Tomato with Parmesan Reggiano 130
    Fried Sweet Plantains 131
    Grilled Plantains 132

Desserts **133**
    Peach Cobbler 135
    Apple Crisp 136
    Arroz con Leche 137
    Tres Leches Cake 138
    Sautéed Pineapple with Rum 140

Happy Hour/Cocktails **141**
    Pina Colada 143
    Frozen Mango Margarita 144
    Frozen Strawberry Daiquiri 145
    Cacique Guaro Sour 146
    Cucumber/Basil Mojito 147

COSTA RICAN CUISINE 101

When we arrived to Costa Rica and settled into our new apartment, we bought all kinds of things we'd never seen before just to experience and experiment. After a few months, we had a decent grasp of the produce. In this book, we fine-tuned our experiments and are bringing to you must have food-hacks and affordable recipes that take full advantage of the amazing produce readily available here.

Our recipes will introduce you to traditional Costa Rican dishes as well as some favorites from home. We embraced the local items such as Lizano Salsa and Tipo Inglesa (a Costa Rican version of worcestershire). By using local items you can cut your grocery budget in half. See the food hacks section for more money saving tips.

We couldn't find pre-made seasonings like blackening spice or taco seasoning, so we just made our versions. Mojo marinade is another thing we love, though it is readily available, we decided to try to make our own. Our version is phenomenal and cost less than half the price of the store-bought brand.

All in all, if you'd like to keep your food costs down, it's very possible. I do admit there are a few cravings we break down and buy at the more expensive import stores. We're cheese nuts, so if I splurge, it's usually on cheese like jalapeño pepper jack.

STAPLE FOODS

The first thing you'll notice about Costa Rican food is that it's fresh, flavorful, and leaves you feeling energetic. While Costa Rican cuisine isn't very spicy, Cholula, Tabasco, and homemade hot chilies are always readily available. You'll see plenty of natural fruit juices, rice, beans, fresh veggies, meat, and salsas often listed on the menu as a *casado*.

Casado literally translates to "married." It's the perfect marriage of foods consisting of white rice, black or red beans, a small side salad, fried plantains, a vegetable side, and a protein (pork, chicken, beef, or fish). As legend has it, the casado played a major role in young courtships. The woman invited her desired spouse over for dinner and cooked a variety of items in order to discover what he liked best. This is why the ingredients in a casado vary a bit from town to town.

Your typical Costa Rican breakfast is healthy and filling. It consists of gallo pinto (Costa Rica's national dish of rice and beans) served with sour cream (natilla), and either scrambled or fried eggs, fried sweet plantains, a slice of ham (jamón), fresh cheese (queso) and of course, world class coffee (café). Some restaurants also include fresh fruit.

Due to the numerous palm plantations, heart of palm (palmito) and palm oil is sold everywhere. A trip to mountainous regions such as Zarcero will lend you to hundreds of handmade signs that proclaim, *"hay queso palmito"* (there is palmito cheese), which is not to be confused with the palmito mentioned above. It's actually a ball of cheese that has a similar texture and taste as string cheese.

If you like fish, you're in for a treat. Costa Rica's coastal communities have numerous top-notch seafood markets to purchase fresh caught tuna (atún), sea bass (corvina), shrimp (camarones), and much more. Most seafood shops also sell homemade ceviche (either mixed seafood or all fish). Ceviche is most certainly a staple food along the coast, usually served with saltine crackers (lime, red onion, and cilantro are predominate flavors). Tabasco is also always nearby.

A popular must-have seasoning in Costa Rican cuisine is [Lizano Salsa](#) (green cap), a mild sauce made from vegetables that is added to everything from meats to gallo pinto. Speaking of food additions, ketchup is much sweeter here so consider yourself forewarned. If you want the ketchup you're accustomed to, simply purchase an American brand in a larger super.

TIP

While pancakes (pankake) aren't Costa Rican in any way, you'll occasionally see them offered on menus. Just know what you'll be served will taste like something between a pancake and a crepe.

SOCK COFFEE

Costa Rican coffee is world class delicious. Every time I visit friends and family at home their singular request is, *"Can you bring me some coffee?"* The coffee is grown along mountains that have tropical sun mixed with cloud forests naturally watering the plants. An ideal environment for a rich smooth flavored coffee (not acidic at all).

The traditional method of brewing the coffee involves a burlap sack (looks a bit like a dirty sock) held up with a ring and hot water from a kettle. The coffee is placed in the sack and the hot coffee is poured over the top. it takes a few minutes to seep through the bag allowing the coffee time to blend it's flavors with the near boiling water.

EGGS

Eggs are a staple in most cultures. One of the first things you'll notice when walking in a super in Costa Rica is the eggs are left out on the shelf, not a' one is refrigerated. As North Americans, we're usually baffled by this and wonder if we're going to get salmonella. Actually, the eggs are very safe and much more natural than those sold in the US. When hens lay their eggs, they're encased with a protecting coat. Only when the eggs are washed (like in the US) do they lose this coating and become more porous creating the need for refrigeration to avoid salmonella. Many countries opt to let mother nature protect the eggs and save the money that would otherwise be drained along with the water required to wash and refrigerate said eggs.

Salmonella can be passed into the egg through infected ovaries of the laying hen (which would carry over regardless of the to wash or not to wash argument), so I wouldn't recommend eating any raw eggs. Costa Rica reports the most common cause of salmonella is through making and consuming homemade mayonnaise.

PRODUCE

Produce in Costa Rica is AMAZING! There's a huge selection of fruits and vegetables. Even though Costa Rica is roughly the size of West Virginia, it holds over 5% of the world's biodiversity (including plants). Many fruits and vegetables will look foreign to you. Other foods you're accustomed to buying aren't readily available or are very expensive due to import fees. Not to worry, part of the reason we wrote this cookbook is to show you "food-hacks" to use in substitution.

For instance, lemons are hard to find but a lemon/lime hybrid that looks more like an ugly wort-ridden lime is readily available, and it actually tastes more like a lemon than a lime. To make it weirder, the inside is orange. To sum it up, buy the ugly lime-looking fruit that taste like lemon and look like an orange. Yellow summer squash is also hard to find, but a great replacement is the chayote. A squash that resembles a giant green walnut. It has a firm flesh and is sweet and slightly tart. It's great in soups and stews because you can cook it for hours and it will still retain its flavor and shape.

Costa Rica is the motherland of fruits. There are pineapples, mangos, papaya, momones chinos (lychee), oranges, guanabana, guava, star fruit, limes, bananas, plantains, kiwi, apples, coconuts, passion fruit, watermelon, strawberries (near Poás), and scores of others, all fresh and at very reasonable prices.

There are local produce stands on almost every street in town. My favorite way to shop is by visiting the local *"feria"* or farmers market on the weekends. There, you are afforded the best pricing, can sample each stand's produce, and buy locally. You can also visit the local *mercado,* which is like a permanent farmers market on steroids and is usually inside an open-air building so you can shop rain or shine. In addition to produce, you can buy freshly butchered meats, homemade tortillas, and fresh made cheese. Feel free to shop all day because there are usually a variety of food stands serving up hot food to order.

One important consideration when buying produce is it doesn't last as long as in the States. The foods aren't sprayed with preservatives, and they're picked when ripe. That, in combination with the heat and humidity, equate short shelf life. Most items need to be eaten within 1-3 days. It's a good thing local markets are always close by. One rule of thumb I've used is "If you buy it refrigerated, keep it refrigerated, if you buy it at room temp, keep it at room temp." Some expats opt to enjoy a morning walk to the market to pick up the food for the day. Others stock up on produce every two-three days.

How to choose the best produce is essential, which is why we're going to teach you.

PICKING PRODUCE 101

Mango

The mangos in Costa Rica are unreal! As they begin to grow on trees across the country, I dance with excitement. The only drawback is the rotten smell of hundreds of mangos that have fallen in the streets. There are many varieties of mangos, but in Costa Rica you primarily see only one type: an enormous oblong softball-sized red/green colored delight.

When choosing your mango, your first lesson is don't focus on color alone. A red-colored mango is not necessarily ripe. Mangos come in a variety of colors - red, yellow, and green, and all can be ripe. If you have had success picking a nice nectarine, you're half-way there. Squeeze the mango gently. A ripe mango will be slightly soft. If it's firm, it is not ready to eat (you could leave it on your windowsill to let it finish ripening). If it's soft, like avocado soft, it's overly ripe. A ripe mango will also have a "fruity" smell on the stem side of the fruit. When you cut it open, the mango should look glossy. If it's dry, it will be sour.

Now that you have your mango, the next big obstacle is how to cut it! After much research and trial and error, here is what I have found to be the easiest and safest way to peel a mango. First lay your mango on a cutting board with the stem end facing away from you. Now roll the mango onto the thickest side. From the top-center measure to the right about a 1/2 inch (or third of the thickness), and using a non-serrated sharp knife slice down the side of the mango. If you hit something hard, try again a little further from the center. Turn the mango around and repeat on the other side. There are still a few small pieces on the remaining sides, just trim around the seed (hard part). For the nice end cuts, here is the trick! Grab a tall drinking glass; make sure it is good and sturdy. Now hold the sliced piece of mango in the palm of your hand skin down. Take the glass and put the edge just above the peel on the end of the mango. Gently slide the glass pushing down along the skin of the mango, continue all the way to the end of the slice. Now you should have the peel in one hand and the mango inside the glass! Repeat for the other side. Believe me, it is a lot harder to explain how to do it than actually doing it.

Another cool trick to impress visitors is take the two thick end pieces and gently score them four or five times in each directions. You're left with a grid of squares. Now bend the peel inside out, and you will have delicious easy to eat, on the go, bit size mango squares.

Cantaloupe

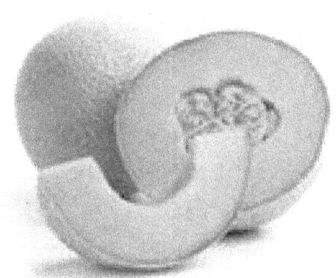

For a sweet tasting cantaloupe, find one with a thorough white-web exterior and a sweet smell from where the stem used to be. If the stem end doesn't have a clean break (partial stem remaining), disregard. The stem on a ripe melon breaks clean when picked. Rub the stem end with your finger as if it were a scratch and sniff sticker. If it doesn't smell sweet, move on to the next one. You don't want the color of the cantaloupe to be very green between the white webbing, rather you're looking for one with an underlying color that is mostly orange/white-ish.

Momones

Momones are also called Lychee in Asia. In Costa Rica, they come in red and yellow varieties. You want to pick a batch that is vibrant in color (pass on any pale looking fruit) and pay special attention to the spikes. Make sure they aren't black or becoming black. When momones turn bad, the first indicator is their hairy (or spiky) parts turn black. For those of you who haven't eaten this fruit, it is delicious and tastes much like grapes. Simply push the nail of your thumb into one, then pull the outer husk apart revealing the pretty grape-like inside. Pop the whole grape-like fruit in your mouth. There is a large seed in the middle that you chew around.

Guava

Bright green guavas aren't ready for consumption. Pick a fruit that is more yellow with pink hues. A ripe guava will have a strong smell, so if you have to place it all the way to your noise in order to smell it, move to the next one. It should smell sweet. Push on the rind, you should feel a slight give.

Star Fruit

Star fruit can be enjoyed as a tart pear-textured fruit or as a sweet grape-like textured fruit. For a tart taste, choose a firm star fruit with a light green tint. For a sweet treat, choose a solid yellow star fruit (or ripen the tart star fruit on your counter for a day or two turning every 12 hours). If the skin on the fruit is mushy, disregard.

Coconut

There are two main applications of coconuts and each one has a preferred type. If you're going to cook with the white "meat," choose an older, larger coconut (*coco* with a yellow/brown exterior). If you want to drink nature's best electrolyte replacement, pick out a rugby-sized green (*pipa*). They are much more refreshing when served ice-cold, so buy one that is sitting in a cooler of ice or fridge ready to be chopped.

Pineapple

Costa Rican pineapple is some of the best I've had in the world. There are a few ways to choose the best pineapple. First look at color and observe the fragrance. You want a pineapple that is more yellow than green on the outer husk. Pick it up and turn it upside. Smell the "butt" of the pineapple, it should be very sweet smelling and lacking signs of mold or rot. The final check involves plucking a few of the leaves off of the top. If they come out easily your pineapple is ready for enjoyment.

Plantains

Plantains can be prepared when they are unripe (green) and when they are ripe (black with a little yellow). If you are hoping to make patacones or other mashed and fried plantain you will likely be using a green plantain. Pay extra attention to the recipe to see which level of ripeness you should buy. In order to pick a ripe plantain, look for one that is 70-90% black with a bit of yellow that also lacks fungal growth (white).

Mangosteen

It's hard to go wrong with mangosteens. When selecting your fruit, look for mangosteens that are firm and have a deep purple color with stems and leaves that are still green. Avoid fruit that is blotchy in color, has brown or yellow leaves, or has a yellow residue, all of which indicate an overripe fruit.

Mangosteen fruit segments similarly to oranges. They often have small pits which are fibrous and a bit sour, so I'd avoid them if I were you.

Papaya

When choosing a papaya, there are three main things to consider. Look for papayas that have more yellow and red and less green. When you squeeze it, is it firm but will give slightly? Can you smell the sweet papaya odor where the stem once was? If you answered yes to each of these questions your papaya is ready for eating or making into a delicious smoothie with milk.

Guanabana

Also called soursop, it is an odd looking fruit with a green spiky peel, white fibrous flesh, and large watermelon-like seeds spattered throughout.

The fruit should be soft when squeezed and smell like a musky version of a pineapple. The spines on the skin should also be on the soft side.

Passion Fruit

Passion fruit are either purple or yellow and when ripe have wrinkly skin. They shouldn't be too lightweight nor hard. The fruit should also have a sweet aroma.

FOOD HACKS

Greek Yogurt

Greek yogurt is super difficult to find in Costa Rica and when you do, you'll pay upwards of $4 for a small serving! We found a way to get our fix without breaking the bank. All you need is a small tupperware dish and either coffee filters or cheese cloth (the former being much easier to find), and a rubber-band, and regular yogurt.
Place the coffee filters over the tupperware and adhere them with a rubber-band (sealing it over the edge of the tupperware. Next, pour your yogurt into the coffee filter. Place your lid on top of the tupperware and refrigerate over night. The following day remove the coffee filter, disregard the water below, and enjoy your greek-styled yogurt.

Worcestershire

Tipo Inglesa runs about $1.70 and has a similar flavor to worcestershire. Actual worcestershire runs about $7!

Ranch Dressing

The ranch dressing commonly found in Costa Rica doesn't taste as you'd expect it to. It's a bit tangy and not as creamy. You can either purchase Kraft Ranch Dressing from a fancy international market for $9 or make our trial and tested homemade ranch (see recipe) which will run you $2.

Mozzarella

Monteverde's white cheese tastes a lot like mozzarella, and when you're on a budget, it's worth the substitution.

TIP
Eat queso fritto (see recipe) to satisfy a cheese craving

Spaghetti

Make your own tomato sauce for your spaghetti recipe. Tomatoes are cheap, simply roast and either mash or puree with sautéed or roasted garlic.

Basic Metric Conversions

In this cookbook we used standard U.S. measurements. Here's a quick guide to converting to metric measurements. For easy reference, we have rounded the equivalent measurements.

WEIGHT

US STANDARD	METRIC
1 oz	30 grams
4 oz	115 grams
8 oz (half a pound)	230 grams
16 oz (1 pound)	460 grams
32 oz (2 pounds)	1 kilogram

VOLUME

US STANDARD	METRIC
1/4 tsp	1.5mL
1/2 tsp	3 mL
1 tsp	5 mL
1 1/2 tsp	7.5 mL
2 tsp	10 mL

US STANDARD	METRIC
1 Tbs	15 mL
1 1/2 Tbs	22.5 mL
2 Tbs	30 mL

US STANDARD	METRIC
1/4 cup	60 mL
1/3 cup	80 mL
2/3 cup	160 mL
3/4 cup	180 mL
1 cup	240 mL

US STANDARD	METRIC
4 cups (1 quart)	1 Liter

OVEN TEMPS

US STANDARD	METRIC
225°F	110°C
250°F	120°C
275°F	135°C
300°F	150°C
350°F	180°C
375°F	190°C
400°F	210°C

Seasonings, Marinades & Dressings

There's a vast array of herbs and spices available in Costa Rica. They're typically sold in small plastic packets for less than a dollar. You can find the American version in 2oz bottles but you'll pay for it. We stumbled across an excellent herb garden call the [Ark Herb Farm](http://www.arkherbfarm.com/)[1] near Poás Volcano. It's a fun and educational tour. They sell over 300 species of medicinal and culinary herbs from around the world. We bought some of our favorites to grow at home. We also pick and dry herbs, saving on the cost and ensuring freshness.

You'll need to brush up on your Spanish when you buy local herbs because many packages don't offer the English translation. I use a translation app and write down the Spanish names of the spices I need before heading to the super. By purchasing small packets of individual spices and mixing your own blends, you can save a bundle. Here are a few of the blends we enjoy.

---

[1] http://www.arkherbfarm.com/

Taco Seasoning

Yields: Approximately – 1 ¼ oz / 40gms
$0.89

- 1 Tbs/7.5gm — Chili Powder/*Chile en Polvo*
- ¼ tsp/.7gm — Garlic Powder/*Ajo Polvo*
- ¼ tsp/.6gm — Onion Powder/*Cebolla Polvo*
- ¼ tsp/.19gm — Crushed Red Pepper Flakes/*Hojuelas de pimiento rojo picado*
- ¼ tsp/.25gm — Dried Oregano/*Orégano seco*
- ½ tsp/1.05gm — Paprika/*Pimentón*
- 1 ½ tsp/3.5gm — Cumin/*Comino*
- 1 tsp/6gm — Sea Salt/*Sal de Mar*
- 1 tsp/2.1gm — Black Pepper/*Pimiento Negro*

Directions:

Combine all ingredients in a small bowl and mix thoroughly. Store in an airtight container for up to six months.

Blackening Spice

Yields: Approximately – 2 oz / 57.7gms

$2.14

- 2 Tbs /13.8gm — Paprika/*Pimentón*
- 2 Tbs/16.8gm — Garlic Powder/*Ajo Polvo*
- 1 Tbs/6.9gm — Onion Powder/*Cebolla Polvo*
- 1 Tbs/6.4gm — Black Pepper/*Pimiento Negro*
- 1 tsp/1.8gm — Cayenne Pepper/*Pimienta de Cayena*
- 1 tsp/1gm — Dried Oregano/*Orégano seco*
- 1 tsp/1gm — Dried Thyme/*Tomillo seco*
- 1 tsp/1.4gm — Cumin/*Comino*
- 1 tsp/2.6gm — Chili Powder/*Chile en Polvo*
- 1 tsp/6gm — Fine Sea Salt/*Sal de Mar*

Directions:

Combine all ingredients in a small bowl and mix thoroughly. Store in an airtight container for up to six months.

Chili Powder

Yields: Approximately – 1 ½ oz / 33.4gms
$1.36

- 2 Tbs/13.8gm   Paprika/Pimentón
- 2 tsp/2gm   Dried Oregano/Orégano seco
- 1 ½ tsp/8.4gm   Garlic Powder/Ajo Polvo
- 1 ½ tsp/2.2gm   Cumin/Comino
- 1 tsp/1.8gm   Cayenne Pepper/Pimienta de Cayena
- ¾ tsp/5.2gm   Onion Powder/Cebolla Polvo

Directions:

Combine all ingredients in a small bowl and mix thoroughly. Store in an airtight container for up to six months.

Citrus Mojo Marinade

Yields: Approximately – 10 oz / 296ml

$1.90

- 3 cloves of Garlic — Minced
- ½ cup /118ml — *Fresh squeezed Orange Juice
- ¼ cup /59ml — *Fresh squeezed Lime Juice
- ¼ cup /59ml — Minced Yellow Onion
- ¼ cup /59ml — Fresh Chopped Cilantro
- ¼ cup /59ml — Extra Virgin Olive Oil
- ½ tsp /1.05gm — Cumin
- ½ tsp /.5gm — Dried Oregano
- ¼ tsp /.75gm — Lemon Pepper
- ¼ tsp /.53gm — Black Pepper
- ½ tsp /1.4gm — Sea Salt (Table salt can be substituted)
- ½ tsp /2.4gm — Hot Sauce (Lizano Tabasco)

Directions:

Combine all ingredients in a jar with a tight-fitting lid. Shake vigorously to mix, refrigerate at least one night before using. This marinade pairs well with Pork, Chicken, Fish, Shrimp and Veggies (especially yucca). Marinate foods in a resealable plastic bag overnight for best flavor.

* You can substitute the juice from sour oranges, use ¾ cup and eliminate both the regular orange and lime juices.

* Variation: eliminate the citrus juice all together and increase olive oil by ½ cup.

Costa Rican Marinade*

Yields: Approximately – 10 oz / 296ml
$1.17

- 2 cloves of Garlic — Minced
- ½ cup/118ml — Fresh squeezed Lime Juice
- ½ tsp/.5gm — Lime zest
- ¼ cup/59ml — Minced Yellow Onion
- 2 Tbs/2gm — Fresh Chopped Cilantro
- 2 tsp/9gm — Extra Virgin Olive Oil
- ¼ cup/59ml — Tomato Juice
- ¼ tsp/.53gm — Black Pepper
- ½ tsp/1.4gm — Sea Salt (Table salt can be substituted)
- 2 Tbs/30ml — Lizano Salsa

Directions:

Combine all ingredients in a jar with a tight-fitting lid. Shake vigorously to mix, refrigerate at least one night before using. This marinade goes great on vegetables, beef, pork, and chicken. Marinate foods in a resealable plastic bag overnight for best flavor.

Ranch Dressing

Yields: Approximately – 14 oz / .4L

$2.19

We searched high and low for a decent ranch dressing in CR. The flavor of the local dressings were quite different from what we're accustomed to in the States. You can buy Kraft® at $9 USD per bottle. This seemed way too steep to us so we decide to make our own. After trying a number of recipes this is the version we settled on. The total cost to make this recipe was less than $2.00 USD.

- ½ cup/118ml — Sour Cream
- 1 cup/237ml — Mayonnaise
- ¼ cup/59ml — Milk
  (Add a little more if you like your Ranch thinner)
- ½ tsp/.4gm — Chives or Green Scallion tops
- ½ tsp/.25gm — Parsley
- 1 Tbs/15 ml — White Vinegar
- ¼ tsp/.6gm — Onion Powder
- ½ tsp/1.4gm — Garlic Powder
- ½ tsp/1gm — Celery Seed or Dill Seed
- ¼ tsp/1.5gm — Fine Salt
- ¼ tsp/.53gm — Black Pepper

Directions:

In a mixing bowl, combine wet ingredients and stir well. In a small bowl, mix all dry ingredients to blend. Sprinkle dry ingredients into mayonnaise mixture a little at a time and mix until blended. Store in an airtight container and refrigerate overnight for flavors to meld.

Batidos, Smoothies, & Refrescos

Basic Batido/Smoothie Recipe

Yields: 2- 8oz glasses

A batido is a smoothie with either a milk or water base. If you order one at a restaurant, that will be their question *"con agua o con leche?"* (with water or with milk?) Each of the following recipes can use a flavored yogurt to help with thickness and serve as a sweetener.

- 2 cups fresh fruit (be creative, mix and match)
- ¼ - ½ cup raw sugar - you can substitute with honey, agave, or stevia
- 1 cup of cold milk – (you can also use water, ice cream, or yogurt)
- Juice from 1 lime, lemon, orange, tangerine etc. (any citrus juice)
- Garnish with fresh fruit slices, fresh mint, herbs, (optional)
- Ice as needed

Directions:

Peel and core your fruit if necessary. Cut into 1" or smaller chunks (makes blending easier), toss into a blender; add sugar, milk, and citrus juice. After blending taste and add additional sweetener to taste. Serve chilled over ice or add ice to the blender for a frozen Batido. Pour into serving glasses and garnish with a slice of fresh fruit.

If you want to increase nutritional value, you can add a variety of veggies: carrot, celery, spinach, or other greens pair well.

Fresh Mango/Banana Batido

Yields: 2- 8oz glasses

$2.54

- 1 large, fresh mango diced into 1" cubes (see produce 101 for advice)
- 1 medium ripe banana
- ¼ - ½ cup raw sugar - you can substitute honey or other sweetener
- 1 cup of cold milk – (you can also use water or yogurt)
- Juice from 1 lime
- Lime slices for garnish (optional)
- Fresh mint (optional)
- Ice as needed

Directions:

Toss into your blender: banana, mango, sugar, milk, and lime juice. Blend well then taste for sweetness. Add additional sweetener as needed. Serve chilled over ice or add ice to the blender for a frozen Batido. Pour into serving glasses and garnish with a lime slice and a mint sprig (if you're trying to impress or are into that sort of thing).

Fresh Strawberry/Banana Batido

Yields: 2- 8oz glasses

$2.16

- 1 pint fresh strawberries (cleaned and topped)
- 1 medium ripe banana
- ¼ - ½ cup raw sugar - you can substitute honey or other sweetener (more if needed)
- 1 cup of cold milk – (you can also use water or yogurt)
- Fresh basil (optional)
- Ice as needed

Directions:

Toss the strawberries and banana into the blender. Add the sugar and milk. Puree and taste. Add additional sweetener as needed. Serve chilled over ice or add ice to the blender for a frozen batido. Pour into serving glasses and garnish with a strawberry and a basil sprig.

Fresh Pineapple/Coconut Batido

Yields: 2- 8oz glasses

$1.98

- 1 pint fresh pineapple (about 1 ½" ring cut from a fresh pineapple and cored)
- ¼ cup fresh or unsweetened coconut
- ¼ - ½ cup raw sugar - you can substitute honey or other sweetener (more if needed)
- 1 cup of cold milk – (you can also use water or yogurt)
- Fresh mint (optional)
- Ice as needed

Directions:

Cut pineapple into 1" chunks, shred fresh coconut or use unsweetened packaged coconut and toss them both into your blender. Add the sugar, milk, and puree. Add additional sweetener to taste. Serve chilled over ice or add ice to the blender for a frozen Batido. Pour into serving glasses and garnish with a pineapple wedge and top with some toasted coconut.

Guanabana Batido

Yields: 2- 8oz glasses

$1.54

Guanabana (also known as soursop) is an odd looking fruit high in vitamin C, B vitamins, and fiber. It has a prickly green outside a white fleshy inside with many inedible black seeds. It's primarily used to make fruit drinks by using the pulp. The fruit has a sweet yet sour taste.

- 1 cup fresh guanabana pulp
- ¼ - ½ cup raw sugar - you can substitute honey or other sweetener (more if needed)
- 1 cup of cold milk – (you can also use vanilla ice cream or yogurt)
- Fresh mint (optional)
- Ice as needed

Directions:

Peel the guanabana and remove the seeds. Add pulp, sugar, and milk to a blender and puree. Add additional sweetener if needed. Serve chilled over ice or add ice to the blender for a frozen Batido. Garnish with lime wedge.

* for a thinner batido strain the fruit

Tamarind Refresco

Yields: a 1/2 Gallon

$2.00

Tamarind is fruit that is commonly proceeded into hard concentrated brown blocks commonly used to make a refreshing juice. It's available at your local produce stand or pulpería (corner store) as a small brown block in plasticwrap.

- 1 Tamarind block
- 2 cups water plus 2 cups
- ½ cup simple syrup - you can substitute honey or other sweetener (more if needed)
- Lime wedge (optional)
- Ice as needed

Directions:

To make tamarind juice, add the tamarind block to 2 cups boiling water. When tamarind is soft, pour mixture through a strainer and press until all liquid is removed. Add simple syrup** and additional 2 cups water. Add more sweetener or water to taste. Serve chilled over ice or add with ice to the blender for a frozen Refresco. Pour into serving glasses and garnish with a lime slice.

** To make simple syrup boil ½ cup sugar in ½ cup water until dissolved.

Salsas, Guacamole, & Appetizers

Olive Oil Dipping Sauce

Yields: 2 servings

$1.82

- ½ cup extra virgin olive oil
- ½ tsp black pepper
- ¼ tsp paprika
- ¼ tsp dried basil
- ¼ tsp dried oregano
- ¼ tsp dried thyme
- ¼ tsp salt
- ¼ tsp garlic powder
- ¼ tsp onion powder
- 1 Tbs parmesan cheese
- Fresh baguette cut into ½" cubes

Directions:

Pour olive oil in a dipping cup add remaining ingredients and stir to mix. Add additional olive oil as needed. Use just enough olive oil to cover spices so you taste a well rounded blend of flavors when dipping.

Fresh Mango & Peach Salsa

Yields: 2-4 servings

$2.50

- 2 large tomatoes (about 1 ½ cups) diced
- 2 peaches diced (about ¾ cup) diced
- ¼ medium mango (about ½ cup) diced
- ½ red onion diced
- ¼ sweet yellow pepper diced
- ¼ red pepper diced
- 3 cloves garlic minced
- ½ tsp cilantro stemmed and chopped
- 1 tsp lime zest
- 1 lime juiced
- Salt to taste
- Optional: 2 Tbs minced jalapeño pepper (more or less depending on how hot you want it)

Directions:

Combine tomatoes, peppers (disregard seeds and juice), onion, peaches, mango, cilantro, and garlic into a medium bowl. Add the remaining ingredients and stir. Add salt and pepper to taste. Chill for at least one hour. It's best served the next day. Serve with tortilla or pretzel chips.

Guacamole

Recipe Courtesy of Shannon Enete
Yields: 4-6 servings

$3.95

- 4 large Hass avocados (aguacates)
- 1/2 cup finely chopped tomato (roma is best, but vine will do.) You want the least amount of juice to enter the guac
- 1/3 cup finely chopped red onion (the finer the chop the better)
- The juice of one lime (lemon-lime hybrid that is abundant in CR)
- Kosher or sea salt to taste (usually about 2 tsp)

* Optionally, add 3-4 cloves of roasted garlic, cilantro, or jalapeño to taste

Directions:

Slice the avocado long side, twist the two pieces apart (much like separating two parts of an oreo cookie), with your knife lightly chop into the seed, then twist so the seed is freed from the avocado and is on your knife. Transfer to the trash. Score the avocado three or four times in each direction, being careful not to slice through the skin on the bottom. Take a spoon and scoop out the pre-sliced fruit into a large mixing bowl. Do this for all eight sides. Add the finely chopped tomatoes, onion, lemon/lime juice, and salt, and mix into the avocado with your knife (if you use a spoon the avocado becomes mashed, "knife-slicing" in the ingredients keeps the guac chunky). The reason it's important to dice the onions and tomato finely is because the smaller they're cut, the more it spreads to each bit of guac and explodes the flavor! Once the ingredients are mixed in, try the guac with a chip. If it doesn't taste flavorful enough, add a little more lime juice and red onion. It's best served slightly chilled.

Best enjoyed with tortilla or pretzel chips

If you have left over guacamole, the trick to keeping it from turning brown is to use cling wrap. Press the wrap starting in the middle of the guacamole, pressing it down directly on the guac. Pat it down until you reach the sides of the bowl, seal the guac to the side of the bowl, expelling all air. Oxygen is what causes the guacamole to turn brown. If done correctly, your guac will last one more day.

Guacamole with Feta Cheese

Yields: 4 servings
$6.55

- 2 large Haas avocadoes (aguacates) peeled and diced (see our section on peeling an avocado)
- 2 medium ripe tomatoes (tomate)
- 1 small red onion finely chopped
- 2 cloves garlic minced
- 3 Tbs fresh chopped cilantro (You can substitute parsley or celery leaves for a milder version)
- 2 Tbs extra virgin olive oil
- 2 Tbs wine vinegar or veggie vinegar (Veggie vinegar is readily available and has a mild flavor)
- 2 oz crumbled feta cheese (for a little more kick substitute gorgonzola or blue cheese)

Directions:

Combine tomatoes, avocados, onion, garlic and cilantro in a bowl. Stir gently to mix. Add oil and vinegar and mix again. Gently stir in ½ of the feta cheese. Crumble remaining feta on top. Chill for one hour or more. Serve with tortilla or pita chips.

Pico de Gallo

Yields: 2 servings
$1.02

This is a versatile dish. It can be served with tortilla chips as an appetizer, used as a topping for a variety of dishes (including Chifrijo, see our recipe), or added on top of steak, pork, or fish to dial up the flavors.

- 2 large tomatoes (diced into 1/4" pieces and disregard seeds and juice)
- 1 green pepper (same as tomatoes)
- 1 jalapeño pepper chopped (omit if you don't like spicy foods)
- ½ bunch of cilantro (about 5 stalks, stemmed and chopped)
- 1 red onion finely chopped
- 1 tsp lime zest
- 1 clove garlic minced (optional)
- 3 limes
- Salt to taste

Directions:

In a medium bowl combine the first 7 ingredients. Zest and juice the limes and pour over mixture, stir until blended. Chill for a minimum of one hour, however, it is best served the next day.

Stuffed Avocados

Yields: 4 servings

$3.36

- 2 Haas avocados
- Pico de Gallo (see the preceding recipe)

Directions:

Cut avocados in half lengthwise, remove seed, scoop out 3/4 of the flesh leaving 1/4 inch of flesh on the peel for strength.

Dice removed avocado and add to your pica de gallo mixture (see the pico de gallo recipe). Spoon mixture back into avocado shells. Serve with warm tortillas.

Queso Fritto

Yields: 2 servings
Recipe courtesy of Shannon Enete
$2.00

✦4 1/4" thick square slides of Queso Blanco (**para fritar**)
✦tsp of vegetable oil

Directions:

Make sure the cheese is made for frying. It will say para fritar on the wrapper if it has a wrapper. If you're buying a block of cheese homemade in a plastic bag, ask the clerk "es bueno para fritar?" Cut the cheese into 1/4" thick squares. Heat your skillet or cast iron pan on high. I like to put a dab of vegetable oil in the pan to assure the cheese doesn't stick and to assist it to reach temperature, but it's not required. Cook on high heat for 1-2 minutes per side. The cheese should sizzle and bubble a bit. When you flip it, the cooked side should be golden or dark brown. Serve with bread, eggs, or gallo pinto.

TIP
A funny thing about this cheese is, I really don't care for the favor when it's uncooked, but fried I love!

Main Dishes

Chicken / Pollo

Chicken *(pollo)* en Salsa

Yields: 2 servings

$4.66

- 2 Boneless skinless chicken breast halves
- 1 medium red pepper diced
- 1 medium onion diced
- 2 large tomatoes chopped into ½" cubes
- ½ cup Lizano Salsa
- 2 Tbs Wochestershire sauce (or Tipo Inglesa)
- 4 Tbs olive oil or butter
- Salt & pepper to taste

Directions:

Pre-heat a skillet to medium-high heat, add oil or butter. Once hot, add chicken and sear on both sides, remove and plate chicken. In the same pan, add the additional 2 Tbs oil or butter, peppers, and onions and sauté until almost soft. Add tomatoes, Lizano Salsa, and worcestershire and stir to combine. Reduce heat to medium low, add chicken back into the skillet, cover, and cook for 8 to 10 minutes or until tomatoes are soft and chicken is fully cooked. Garnish with a sprig of fresh cilantro.

Pair with
    Costa Rican Rice
    Veggie medley

Rosemary Chicken

Yields: 2 servings

$2.76

- 2 Boneless skinless chicken breast halves
- 2 Tbs Lemon/lime hybrid juice
- 1 Tbs fresh rosemary chopped
- 2 small sprigs of fresh rosemary for garnish
- 2 Tbs butter
- salt & pepper to taste

Directions:

For Marinade: pour lemon/lime juice into a bowl, add fresh chopped rosemary, a dash of salt and pepper, and stir to until mixed. Place chicken breasts into a sealable plastic bag and pour in marinade. Marinate for a minimum of one hour, however, overnight is best.

To Cook: Pre-heat a skillet over medium high heat, add butter and melt. Add chicken and sear on both sides, reduce heat to medium-low, cover and cook for 3 minutes per side. During the last two minutes of cooking, place fresh rosemary sprigs on top of chicken. Serve immediately leaving roasted rosemary on chicken. As an option, you can make gravy out of the pan drippings.

Pair with
  Rice Pilaf
  Wilted kale with tomato and blue cheese

Fried Chicken

Yields: 2 servings

$2.68

- 1 Boneless skinless chicken breast, thigh and leg
- 1 ½ Tbs olive oil
- 1 ½ Tbs butter
- 1 egg slightly beaten
- ½ cup all-purpose flour
- ½ cup breadcrumbs
- salt & pepper to taste

Directions:

Marinating: This receipe can be made with either marinated or unflavored chicken. Try marinating the chicken in the Costa Rican marinade or your favorite Italian Dressing. If you do marinate the chicken, remove excess marinade and pat dry before proceeding.

To Cook: Pre-heat a skillet over medium-high heat, add butter and olive oil. Coat chicken, dredge in flour, and shake off excess flour. Next, dip the chicken into the egg making sure the entire piece of chicken is coated. Shake off excess egg then roll in the breadcrumbs. Add the chicken to your hot skillet and sear on both sides, reduce your heat to medium and cover. Cook for 3 minutes per side. Remove chicken to serving platter. Pour off any extra oil left in pan.

* As an option, you can make gravy out of the pan drippings. Add one cup of chicken broth or bouillon. Bring to a boil, add salt and pepper to taste. Next mix 2 Tbs of all-purpose flour in 2 Tbs of water. Stirring constantly slowly pour flour mixture into gravy a little at a time. Stop when you reach desired consistency. Stir continuously and cook for one minute longer.

Pairings
Mashed Potatoes or Mashed Yucca
Roasted Cauliflower with lime sauce

Seafood

Seared Tuna Steaks with Ginger-Lime Sauce

Yields: 2 servings

$8.06

- 2 Fresh Tuna Steaks (4-6 oz each)
- 2 small bunches of fresh cilantro
- 1 jalapeño pepper seeded and sliced (more or less depending on the amount of heat you like)
- 1 ½ tsp grated fresh ginger
- 2 cloves garlic minced
- 2 limes juiced
- 1/2 tsp lime zest
- 1/3 cup extra virgin olive oil
- 1/2 tsp honey (substitute sugar or other sweetener)
- sea salt and black pepper
- 3 Tbs soy sauce

Directions:

In a mixing bowl, combine the cilantro, jalapeño, ginger, garlic, lime zest, lime juice, soy sauce, honey, salt, pepper and 3 Tbs of olive oil. Stir ingredients together until well blended.

Pre-heat skillet to medium-high heat, add remaining olive oil and coat pan. Sprinkle the tuna with salt and pepper. Sear Tuna for 1 minute on each side, add ½ the ginger-lime sauce to the pan. Cook for 1 minute longer. The inside of the tuna will be red and the outer ¼" on both sides will be white. (If you do not like your tuna red then cook for 2 additional minutes for tuna to be cooked through) Transfer tuna to plates and pour remaining ginger-lime sauce over tuna and serve.

Pairs with

Fresh avocado slices
White rice

Baked Tilapia

Yields: 2 servings

$6.72

- 2 medium tilapia fillets
- 2 cups Costa Rican rice (see recipe)
- 1 ½ cups prepared black beans with black water, fresh or canned.
- 1 cup fresh pineapple diced
- 1 cup salsa fresh or jarred
- 2 Tbs cilantro chopped or parsley
- 1 lime sliced

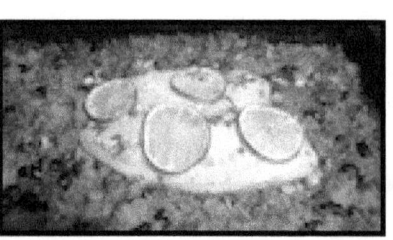

For Marinade:
- ¼ cup orange juice
- 1 lime, juiced
- 1 tsp lime zest
- 2 Tbs olive oil
- 2 Tbs cilantro or parsley chopped
- 2 cloves of garlic chopped
- 1 tsp sugar
- Salt & pepper to taste

Directions:

In a small bowl combine all ingredients for marinade, stir until sugar is dissolved. Rinse fillets under cool water, pat dry with paper towels. Place fillets in a zipper type plastic bag, pour in marinade and seal. Flip bag to make sure fish is fully coated with marinade. Marinate for 1 hour in refrigerator. Meanwhile, prepare *Costa Rican rice* per recipe. When rice has cooled, in a large bowl combine 2 cups of rice, black beans, pineapple, salsa, cilantro, and salt and pepper to taste, stir to combine. Pour mixture into 13" by 9" baking dish. Place marinated fillets on top, then pour marinade over the entire dish, add thinly sliced limes on top. Bake at 400° for 25 to 30 minutes or until the fish is flaky.

Blackened Corvina

Yields: 2 servings

$6.32

- 2 medium corvina fillets (White Sea Bass)
- 2 Tbs of Blackening Spice (See recipe in the spice section)
- 3 Tbs butter

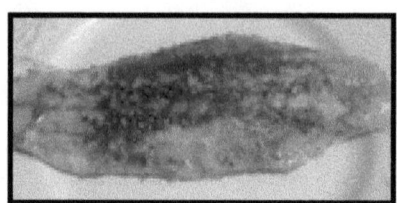

Directions:

Rinse fillets under cool water, pat dry with paper towels. Melt butter in microwave or small pan on stove. Pour butter in a flat dish with sides. Dip corvina into butter coating then thoroughly sprinkle with blackening spice. Repeat for the 2nd fillet. For a spicier fish, add extra blackening spice. Add the remaining butter to your skillet and heat on high. Once your skillet is hot, reduce to medium-high and place both fillets in the pan seasoned side down. Add spices to other side of fillets. Sear fish for 3 minutes, carefully turn fish over and sear another 2 minutes. Serve immediately.

Pairs with
Rice Pilaf

Shrimp Etouffee

Yields: 4 servings

$12.96

- 1 lb medium shrimp (cleaned and deveined)
- ¼ cup extra virgin olive oil plus 2 tbs
- ¼ cup all-purpose flour
- 1 medium red pepper sliced into 2" x ¼" pieces
- 1 medium green pepper (sliced as above)
- 1 medium yellow pepper (sliced as above)
- 1 medium red onion (you can substitute white or yellow, sliced as above)
- 3 cloves garlic minced
- 2 stalks celery chopped into ½" pieces
- 2 large tomatoes diced
- 1 cup dry red wine
- 1 cup chicken, vegetable or fish stock
- 2 Tbs red wine vinegar
- 4 Tbs butter
- 2 Tbs fresh basil chopped (2 tsp dry)
- 2 Tbs fresh oregano (2 tsp dry)
- 2 Tbs fresh thyme (2 tsp dry)
- 1 tsp salt
- 1 tsp black pepper

Directions:

Add 2 Tbs of olive oil and 2 Tbs of butter to a large skillet over medium heat. Add garlic and sauté until garlic is fragrant (2 to 3 minutes). Add shrimp and sauté an additional 2 to 3 minutes, just until pink (shrimp will finish cooking later). Remove shrimp and set aside. Add remaining olive oil to skillet increase to medium-high heat. Whisk in flour, turn heat down to medium and cook, stirring constantly until it gives off a nutty aroma (about 10 to 15 minutes).

Add veggies and sauté until soft but very al dente. Add wine, stock, vinegar, tomatoes and spices, and stir until thickened. Add salt and pepper to taste. Reduce heat to low and add shrimp back to skillet. Add remaining butter and sauté until shrimp are fully cooked. Serve over white rice.

Beef

Jojo's Meatloaf

Yields: 3-4 servings

$6.12

- 1 ½ lbs ground beef (I like 90% for meatloaf)
- 1 small onion diced
- ¼ red pepper diced
- 3 Tbs celery diced
- 2 pcs bread dried and crumbled or 3/4 cup breadcrumbs
- 1 egg slightly beaten
- 1 Tbs catsup
- 1 Tbs worcestershire sauce (salsa Tipo Inglesa)
- 1 tsp mustard
- 2 Tbs butter
- ½ tsp Lizano Tabasco
- 2 Tbs parmesan cheese
- ½ tsp garlic powder
- ½ tsp black pepper
- ½ tsp salt

Glaze
- ½ cup catsup
- 1 tsp brown sugar
- ¼ tsp dry mustard (or yellow mustard)
- Dash of Lizano Tabasco

Directions:

Add butter to a skillet over medium-high heat. Add onion, red pepper and celery, stir for 5 to 6 minutes to remove moisture. Set aside and let cool. Mix egg, catsup, worcestershire, mustard, tabasco, parmesan cheese, garlic, salt, and pepper in a medium size bowl. Add hamburger, breadcrumbs and veggies to bowl. Mix with your hands until combined. Don't over mix because it will make meatloaf tough. Form into a loaf and place on a baking sheet. Bake at 375° for 30 to 40 minutes. While baking, mix your glaze. Remove meatloaf from the oven with 15 minutes left to cook and apply glaze. Return to oven. If you have extra glaze reapply glaze after 5 minutes. Let meatloaf rest 5 to 7 minutes before cutting.

Shepherd's Pie

Yields: 4 servings

$8.28

- 1 ½ lbs ground beef (I like 90%)
- 4 Tbs olive oil or butter
- 2 cloves garlic minced
- 1 small onion diced
- ½ red pepper diced
- 1 stalk celery finely diced
- 2 Tbs worcestershire sauce
- 1 small can tomato paste
- ½ cup dry red wine
- ¾ cup chicken or beef stock
- 1 Tbs rosemary
- 1 tsp basil
- 1 tsp oregano
- 1 tsp thyme
- Salt and pepper to taste

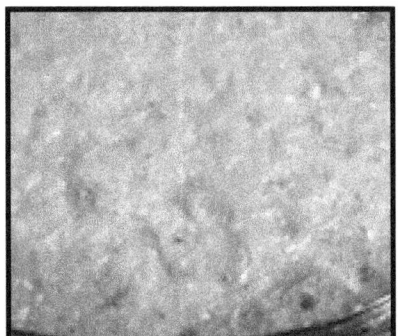

Topping:

- 1 ½ lbs potatoes peeled and cut into chunks
- 2 Tbs butter
- 2 scallions finely chopped
- 2 to 4 Tbs milk
- ¾ cup grated cheddar cheese
- Salt and pepper to taste

Directions:

Pre-heat oven to 350°. In a skillet, brown ground beef in 2 Tbs of olive oil and set aside. In the same skillet, add the remaining 2 Tbs of olive oil and cook onion and peppers for approximately 6 minutes over medium heat until soft. Stir in worcestershire sauce and tomato paste. Add browned beef and wine and scrape the bottom of skillet to loosen taste bits. Cook a few minutes to cook off the alcohol. Add stock and bring to a boil. Reduce heat to medium-low and add spices. Cook for 10 minutes to reduce liquid and blend flavors. Set aside to cool.

Meanwhile, boil the potatoes until soft. Drain and mash until smooth. Stir in butter, salt, and pepper. (If it's too stiff, add some milk to thin.) Fold in ½ of the cheese and mix. Pour beef mixture into 13" x 9" casserole dish. Top with mashed potatoes and sprinkle remaining cheese on top. Cook 15 to 20 minutes or until potatoes are browned and mixture bubbles along the edge. Serve and enjoy!

Breaded Bistec Steak

Yields: 4 servings

$5.12

- 1 lb or 2 pcs marinated bistec steak
- ½ cup breadcrumbs
- 1 egg
- ¼ cup flour
- 2 Tbs olive oil or butter

Marinated bistec (skirt steak) is available at most butcher shops. If you can't find marinated steaks see our recipe for *"Costa Rican Marinade."* Prepare marinade and marinate steaks overnight.

Directions:

Heat olive oil or butter in a large skillet over medium heat. In a bowl, whip egg in until yoke and egg white are combined. Coat steaks with flour and shake off excess. Dip the steak into the whipped egg then dredge in breadcrumbs. Fry steaks until golden brown. Plate and serve topped with our pica de gallo recipe.

Pairs with
 Mojo yucca
 Squash Hash

Sloppy Joe's

Yields: 4 servings

$4.80

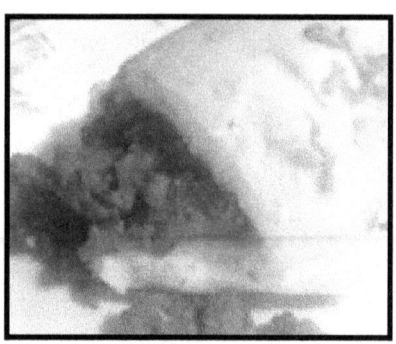

- 1 lb ground beef
- ½ green bell pepper finely diced
- ½ red bell pepper finely diced
- ¼ yellow bell pepper finely diced
- ¼ medium onion diced
- ½ cup tomato sauce
- ½ cup catsup
- 2 Tbs worcestershire sauce
- 2 Tbs Lizano Salsa
- Dash of tabasco sauce
- ½ tsp garlic powder
- ½ tsp onion powder
- Salt & pepper to taste
- 2 Tbs olive oil or butter

Directions:

Heat olive oil or butter in a large skillet over medium heat. Brown ground beef and drain excess grease, then set aside. In the same skillet add peppers and onion and sauté until tender. Reduce heat to low and add meat back to skillet. Add the remaining ingredients and cook over low heat for ten minutes to blend flavors. Serve on fresh Costa Rican bread.

Pairs with
French fries/ Yucca Fries
Coleslaw

Ameri-Rican Stew

Yields: 6 servings

$6.85

We call this American / Costa Rican Stew due to the vegetables that are readily available here in Costa Rica. The main ingredient in this recipe is the Chayote. This is a wonderful vegetable in the squash family. It has a great flavor and holds its shape and texture even after cooking for extended periods of time. The second key ingredient is Lizano Salsa. It's a staple in Costa Rican homes and is used on everything.

- 1 ½ lbs stew beef (with some bones is preferred but add ½ lbs for bones)
- 2 cups beef stock
- ½ cup dry red wine
- 2 large white potatoes cut into chunks or 6 small
- ¼ head of white cabbage cut into strips
- ¼ head of red cabbage cut into strips
- 1 medium yellow onion coarsely chopped
- 1 medium carrot sliced into rounds
- 2 stalks celery sliced
- 1 small zucchini sliced
- 1 red pepper sliced into 2" strips
- 2 ears of corn cut into 2" pieces
- ½ small chayote peeled and diced into ½" cubes
- 2 medium tomatoes diced
- 3 cloves of garlic roughly chopped
- 1 tsp onion powder
- 1 tsp thyme
- 2 tsp basil
- 1 tsp oregano
- 1 tsp salt (to taste)

- 1 tsp black pepper (to taste)
- 2 Tbs Lizano Salsa

Directions:

Pre-heat your skillet on Med-High heat and add 2 Tbs of olive oil. Sear the beef on each side, then reduce the heat to low and add the rest of the ingredients. Stir your stew then cover. Cook the mixture on low heat for 2 hours or until meat and veggies are tender, stirring occasionally.

Jojo's Spaghetti with Albendingas (Meatballs)

Yields: 6-8 servings

$7.96

Meatballs:

- 1 lb ground beef
- 2 Tbs green onion with tops minced
- 2 Tbs fresh oregano chopped or 1 tsp dried
- 1 Tbs fresh parsley or ½ tsp dried
- 1 clove garlic minced
- 1 tsp worcestershire sauce
- 2 Tbs of vegetable oil
- ¼ cup breadcrumbs

Marinara Sauce

- 5 large tomatoes peeled and crushed
- ¼ cup extra virgin olive oil
- 2 cloves garlic minced
- 1 small onion minced
- 1 celery stalk minced
- 1 small carrot minced
- ½ cup red wine
- 2 Tbs fresh basil or 1 tsp dried
- 2 Tbs fresh oregano or 1 tsp dried
- 2 Tbs fresh thyme or 1 tsp dried
- 1 Tbs fresh parsley or ½ tsp dried
- 1 bay leaf
- 1 Tbs honey
- ½ tsp red pepper flakes
- ½ tsp sea salt
- ½ tsp black pepper

Directions:
Sauce

If you're going to puree the sauce you don't have to peel your tomatoes, simply cut out the cores and chop into ½ inch pieces. If you like chunkier sauces, then you'll have to peel the tomatoes. Here is a trick to easy peeling: cut an x on top of the tomatoe then drop in boiling water for 10 seconds. Quickly remove and drop in ice water. The skin will peel right off.

Dice tomatoes into ½ inch pieces. Pre-heat skillet on Med-High heat, add onions, garlic, celery and carrots and cook for 15 minutes. Add tomatoes, bay leaf, wine, basil, thyme, oregano, parsley and honey. Simmer 2 to 3 hours over very low heat, stirring occasionally. During the last hour, add your meatballs. Add salt & pepper to taste, remove bay leaf and serve over pasta of your choice.

For Meatballs:

In a large mixing bowl add ground beef, onion, oregano, parsley, garlic, and worcestershire sauce. Mix until just combined (over mixing will make meatballs dense and heavy). Fold in breadcrumbs until incorporated. Form into meatballs (whatever size you prefer) then place in a shallow pan, cover with plastic wrap, and refrigerate for 30 minutes. Afterwards, heat vegetable oil in a large skillet over medium high heat, cook meatballs until browned and mostly cooked through.

Pairs with:

Garden salad

**This recipe is a great appetizer. Just make the meatballs about ¾ of an inch in size and serve them in the marinara sauce in a slow cooker.

Pork

Stuffed Pork Sirloin Tip Roast

Yield: 6 servings

$9.30

- 1 ½ to 2 lbs. pork sirloin tip roast
- ¼ medium onion finely diced
- ¼ red pepper finely diced
- 3" of celery diced
- 1 clove garlic
- 2 oz cheese of your liking grated
- ¼ cup breadcrumbs
- 2 Tbs butter plus 2 Tbs
- ½ tsp basil
- ½ tsp oregano
- ½ tsp thyme
- ½ tsp black pepper
- ½ tsp salt
- Kitchen twine for tying roast
- ¾ cup water plus 2 Tbs
- 2 Tbs flour

Directions:

To prep you roast start with a sharp knife. Lay the roast on the cutting board with the longer side facing away from you. Make an incision approximately ½ inch deep, slicing down (toward cutting board). Then cut parallel to the cutting board. When you're done you should have a ½ inch thick slab of pork. In a skillet melt butter and add onion, pepper, celery and garlic. Sauté over medium heat until onion is translucent (about 5 minutes). Stir in breadcrumbs and spices and sauté another minute. Remove from stove and set aside. Next, spoon mixture to cover the entire roast, and add grated cheese. Starting at one end of the roast, roll the meat into a log, tuck any extra stuffing that may fall out into roast. Cut a 2 foot piece of kitchen twine. Lift roast and lay string under about 1" from end and tie a snug knot. Continue to wrap string around roast spacing about 1 ½" apart per wrap. When you reach the other end make final wrap about 1" from end and tie a 2nd knot. Season the outside liberally with salt and pepper. To cook, preheat a medium stock pot on medium-high heat. Add 2 Tbs of butter and sear roast on all sides about 1 to 2 minutes per side. Reduce heat to low, cover, and cook roast for 30 minutes or until a meat thermometer reads 150°F. Cook longer if needed. When the roast is at temperature (check in 2 or more places) remove and place on a serving tray to rest. While it's resting, add ¾ cup water to stock pot and bring to boil. Using a wooden spoon loosen all pan drippings. In a cup add 2 Tbs cold water and 2 Tbs of flour and stir until smooth. With the stock pot water boiling add flour mixture a little at a time stirring continuously until desired thickness. Add salt and pepper to taste. Remove gravy from the heat. Cut and remove twine from roast. Slice and arrange on a serving platter. Spoon gravy over roast and serve.

Mojo Marinated Pork Chops

Yields: 2 servings

$4.72

- 2 - ½ lb pork chops
- 3 to 5 oz of mojo marinade (see recipe)
- 2 Tbs butter or oil

Directions:

Trim pork chops of excess fat, leaving a little for flavor. Place the chops into a plastic sealable bag, add mojo marinade and seal the bag squeezing out as much air as possible. Place in a pan (just in case of leaks) and place in the refrigerator. Marinate at least 2 hours, but overnight is always better.

In a large skillet, heat butter or oil over medium-high heat. Add pork chops (retain marinade) and sear both sides about 2 minutes per side. Bring the heat down to low, cover, and cook the chops for 6 to 8 minutes turning once. Remove chops to serving platter, cover, and let rest at least 5 minutes. Meanwhile, return the heat of your skillet to medium-high, pour remaining marinade into the skillet then add ½ cup water and bring to boil. Cook for 3 to 4 minutes, add salt and pepper to taste. (Sauce can be thickened by adding 2 Tbs of cornstarch to 2 Tbs of cold water, mix thoroughly and slowly pour into sauce stirring continuously for 2 minutes or until thickened.)

Pairs with

Mashed potatoes
Cooked cabbage BBQ

Pulled Pork Sliders

Yields: 4 servings

$6.84

Cook-time: 4 to 5 hours

- 1 ½ lbs boneless pork roast
- 3 oz of mojo marinade (see recipe)
- 2 cups chicken broth
- 1 small onion minced
- 2 cloves garlic minced
- 1 cup barbecue sauce
- ¼ cup Lizano Salsa
- ¼ cup worcestershire sauce
- Salt and pepper to taste

Directions:

Heat a stock-pot over medium heat, add all ingredients *except the pork* and stir to combine. Cut pork into 2" pieces and add to the pot. Cover and simmer on low heat for 4 to 5 hours or until pork falls apart when touched with a fork. Using a fork and wooden spoon break pork apart. If it's too juicy, turn the heat up to medium and cook uncovered for 15 minutes more to reduce liquid. Taste and add additional barbecue sauce if needed. Serve on local fresh Costa Rican bread from your panadería.

Chicharrón Cerdo*

Recipe Courtesy of **Carniceria Solo Bueno**
Yields: 4 servings

$5.08

- 2 lbs pork boneless skirt or rib meat
- 1 ½ garlic bulbs peeled and roughly chopped
- 3 Tbs vegetable oil (for pan sear), or 1 quart to fill deep fryer
- 1 tsp salt
- 2 oz soy sauce
- 3 oz salsa tipo inglesa (worcestershire sauce)

Chicharron Cerdo is chunks of pork deep fried and is a staple dish in Costa Rica. The traditional cooking method is deep frying in lard! The flavors are wonderful. We've also prepared it on the stove top with no added oil in our HealthCraftCR cookware.

Directions:

In a mixing bowl, combine the garlic, salt, soy sauce and worcestershire sauce, and mix until blended. Next, slice your meat into 2" x 2" pieces. Add the meat to a 1 gallon zipper top plastic bag and pour in your mixture. Marinate meat for at least 4 hours, but overnight is best.

For Deep Frying: Pre-heat oil to 350°, deep fry meat in batches to keep oil hot. Cook for 6 to 8 minutes or until meat is deep brown. To test, remove one piece of meat and slice in half, if thoroughly cooked remove the rest of the meat. If not, return cut meat to deep fryer and continue to cook until done.

For Pan Searing: Pre-heat skillet to medium-high heat, (if you don't have HealthCraftCR cookware) add 3 Tbs of vegetable oil and coat pan. Sear the meat on all sides then cook on medium heat for 8 to 10 minutes turning occasionally. Do not crowd the pan with meat, if necessary cook in two batches.

If you have HealthCraftCr cookware, preheat your skillet to medium-high heat without oil! Sear meat on all sides. Meat will stick to pan when first added and will release when ready to turn. Once all of the meat is seared, reduce heat to low and cover with vent open. Cook for 7 to 9 minutes or until desired doneness is achieved.

Pairs with

Yucca Hash
Veggie Medly

Vegetarian

Thai Stir-fry

Yields: 4 servings

$3.16

This dish is very versatile, experiment with any veggies you'd like, below is a list of what I used. The recipe changes nearly every time we make it. We just use what we have on hand.

- ¼ chayote chopped into ½ inch cubes
- ¼ red pepper sliced into strips
- ¼ green pepper sliced into strips
- ½ cup green cabbage chopped
- ½ cup red cabbage chopped
- ½ cup mushrooms sliced
- ½ cup onions sliced
- ½ cup carrots sliced
- ½ cup broccoli flowerets
- 2 Tbs butter or olive oil
- 1 clove garlic minced
- ½ cup vegetable broth or chicken broth
- ½ cup oyster sauce
- 2 Tbs fish sauce
- 1 Tbs turmeric
- ½ Tbs fresh ginger minced
- Salt & pepper to taste

Directions:

In a large skillet with lid (wok works best) add butter or oil and heat over medium heat. Add garlic and ginger, sauté until fragrant. Add all veggies and stir fry until slightly wilted. Add broth, spices, salt and pepper, cover and lower heat to low. Cook 5 minutes, stir and add oyster sauce and fish sauce (if you can't find fish sauce you can omit but it is better with it). Cook uncovered an additional 5 minutes to thicken sauce. Serve over rice or noodles.

Variations: Add chicken, beef, pork, shrimp, etc. Start by stir-frying meat in butter or olive oil with 1 clove of garlic over medium high heat. Only cook halfway about 3 to 4 minutes. Remove from pan and set aside. Continue with recipe above, after you add broth, add meat back to skillet and continue finishing steps.

No Crust Feta & Kale Quiche

Yields: 4 servings

$7.96

- 5 eggs
- 1 cup milk
- ½ cup chopped kale
- ¼ cup chopped onion
- 4 oz feta cheese
- 2 Tbs cheddar cheese shredded
- 1 Tbs olive oil
- 1 Tbs butter
- ½ tsp thyme plus ½ tsp
- ¼ tsp lemon zest plus ¼ tsp
- ½ tsp salt
- ½ tsp black pepper

Directions:

Preheat oven to 350°. Combine egg then milk and whisk until blended, set aside. In a skillet, add olive oil and butter and melt over medium heat. Add onions and kale, sauté until onions are softened and kale is wilted, about 3 to 4 minutes. Set aside to cool. Crumble feta cheese into egg mixture, then add thyme, lemon zest, salt and pepper and whisk until well blended. Pour into skillet and mix. Pour mixture into a 9" pie pan, sprinkle with cheddar cheese and remaining thyme and lemon zest. Bake until top is lightly browned, about 40 minutes.

Vegetarian Lasagna

Yields: 4 – 6 servings

$8.84

- 1 box lasagna noodles
- 4 – 5 leaves of kale stemmed and torn into bite sized pieces or substitute with 1 ½ cups spinach leaves
- 2 stalks celery diced
- ½ red pepper diced
- ½ yellow pepper diced
- 1 medium onion diced
- 4 slices 5" squash cut into quarters
- ½ carrot shredded
- ½ eggplant sliced into rounds and quartered
- (Add any veggies you like)
- 1 lb mozzarella cheese shredded
- 1 cup ricotta cheese
- 1 cup mild young queso
- 2 cups marinara sauce (see recipe under spaghetti and meatballs)

Directions:

Preheat oven to 350°. Prepare lasagna noodles per directions on the box. Once noodles are ready, grease a 2" x 9" x 13" baking pan and spoon ¼ cup of marinara into pan. Add a layer of noodles, overlap if needed. Spoon ½ cup of marinara sauce over noodles, add a layer of vegetables followed by all three cheeses. Repeat for second and third layers. Before adding the final layer of cheese, spoon any leftover marinara sauce over veggies then top with cheeses. Shred some parmesan cheese on top and place your creation in the oven. Bake at 350° for 30 to 45 minutes or until top is nicely browned and sauce is bubbly. Remove from the oven and let cool for 10 minutes before cutting.

Eggplant Parmesan

Yields: 4 servings

$5.12

- 1 large eggplant
- ½ lb mozzarella cheese
- ½ cup grated parmesan cheese
- 10 fresh basil leaves or 2 Tbs dried basil
- ½ cup breadcrumbs
- 1 ½ cups marinara sauce (see Jojo's spaghetti and albóndigas for recipe)

Directions:

Preheat oven to 400°, slice eggplant in ½" thick slices and place on a greased sheet pan. Bake for 8 to 12 minutes or until eggplant starts to turn brown. Remove from oven and set aside to cool. Lower oven temperature to 350°. In a 13" x 9" baking dish, spread 6 of the largest slices of eggplant evenly, add ½ of the marinara sauce, ¼" thick slice of mozzarella cheese, ½ of the basil, grated parmesan cheese and ½ the breadcrumbs. Add a 2nd layer of eggplant and repeat, finish with the breadcrumbs and a little extra parmesan cheese. Bake the dish for 20 minutes uncovered until breadcrumbs are nicely browned.

Pairs with

Kale and tomato salad
Pasta

Stuffed Chayote

Yields: 4 servings

$6.56

- 2 medium chayote squash
- 1 medium onion diced
- ½ medium red pepper diced
- 2 cloves garlic minced
- ½ cup plus ¼ cup grated parmesan cheese
- 1 cup breadcrumbs
- 1 egg beaten
- 2 Tbs butter or olive oil
- 2 Tbs cilantro or parsley

Directions:

Place chayote in a pot and cover with water, add salt, boil chayote 12 to 15 minutes or until soft. When cool enough to handle, cut in half and remove seed. Scoop out the flesh leaving about ¼" along shell for support. Turn shells up-side down to drain. Chop pulp and place in a bowl for later.

Preheat oven to 350°

Heat butter in a skillet over medium high heat, add garlic, onions and red pepper, sauté for 3 to 4 minutes. Add mushrooms and sauté until mushrooms release there liquid, about 3 to 4 minutes. Remove from heat and stir in remaining ingredients less the ¼ cup extra parmesan cheese. Add reserved chayote pulp with its liquid, stir to combine. Spoon mixture into chayote shells, drizzle with a little melted butter and remaining ¼ cup parmesan cheese. Bake for 20 to 25 minutes or until topping is lightly browned.

Pairs with

Tomato Caprese salad

Soups

Chili Con Carne with Beans

Yields: 6 servings

$10.14

- 1 lbs ground beef
- 4 large ripe tomatoes (chopped into ½" cubes)
- 3 cups chicken or beef stock
- ½ cup dried red beans washed and soaked overnight (omit if you don't like beans in your Chili)
- ½ cup dry white beans washed and soaked overnight (omit if you don't like beans in your chili)
- 1 small can of tomato paste
- 1 9 oz bag of Santa Cruz Medio Chunky Salsa
- 1 large red pepper diced
- 1 medium yellow onion diced
- 1 small jalapeño pepper seeded and minced (more or less depending on how hot you like it)
- 3 cloves garlic minced
- 2 Tbs chili powder **
- 2 Tbs fresh chopped basil (2 tsp dried)
- 2 Tbs fresh chopped oregano (2 tsp dried)
- 2 Tbs fresh thyme (2 tsp dried)
- 1 Tbs paprika
- 1 Tsp cumin
- 1 tsp cayenne
- 1 tsp salt
- 1 tsp black pepper

Directions:

Brown ground beef, add onions, peppers and garlic then sauté for 2 minutes. Add broth, tomatoes, paste and salsa. Stir until combined, add spices. Simmer on low heat for 2 to 4 hours. Taste and adjust spices as needed. As always with soups and stews it's even tastier the next day! Serve with grated cheese and sour cream.

** See our recipe to make your own!

Garbanzo Bean Soup

Yields: 6 servings

$6.00

- 1 bag 500gm dried garbanzo beans
- 3 large potatoes
- 1 ½ packets of Sazon Goya con azafran
- 1 medium onion coarsely chopped
- 4 oz salt pork or bacon
- 4 oz mexican chorizo (this is hard to find so substitute any good chorizo)
- Salt and pepper to taste

Directions:

Soak garbanzo beans in salted water overnight, rinse and add to an 8 qt stock pot. Add water to cover about 1" over beans. Bring to a boil and boil for one hour. Add remaining ingredients except potatoes, reduce heat to low and simmer for 3 to 4 hours more. Add potatoes and cook until tender.

Vegetable Beef Soup

Yield: 6 servings

$7.25

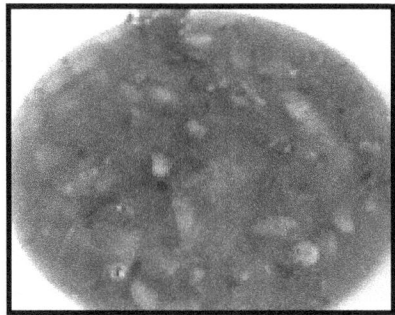

- 1 lb chuck roast cut into 1" cubes
- 1 medium onion coarsely chopped
- 2 carrots chopped
- 2 celery stalks chopped
- 1 large tomato diced
- 1 packets of Sazon Goya con azafran
- 2 Tbs butter
- Salt and pepper to taste
- 1½ quarts water

Directions:

In a large stock pot, sear beef in 1 Tbs of butter over medium-high heat. Cook in small batches for 4 to 5 minutes, turning frequently. When beef is done remove to a plate and repeat until all beef is seared. Add the remaining Tbs of butter to your pan and sauté onions, carrots, and celery (about 5 minutes), or just until softened. Return beef and juices to the pot, add water and bring to a boil, reduce heat to medium low and cover, cook for one hour. Add tomato, parsley, Sazon, salt and pepper. Simmer for an additional 20 minutes then serve.

Quick Chicken Noodle Soup

Yields: 2 servings

$3.76

- ½ lb boneless chicken breast cut into ½ " cubes
- 3 cups water
- ¼ cup carrots shredded
- ¼ cup celery stalks finely chopped
- 3 chicken bouillon cubes
- 1 packet of Sazon Goya con azafran
- Salt and pepper to taste

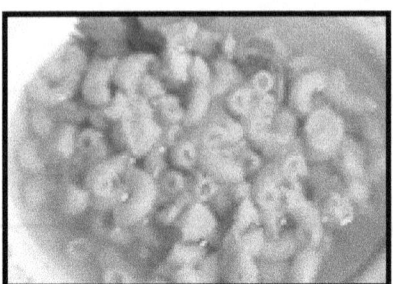

Directions:

In a small stock pot add water, bouillon, and sazon and bring to a boil. Add chicken and cook over high heat about 4 to 5 minutes. Remove chicken to a bowl. Add pasta, carrots, and celery then bring back to a boil and cook 8 minutes or until pasta is al dente. Add the chicken back to your pot and reduce heat to low, simmering for 10 minutes. Add salt and pepper to taste.

Salads

Cucumber/Orange/Tomato Salad

Yields: 2 servings

$3.02

+ 1 medium cucumber (sliced thin and uniform)
+ 6 cherry tomatoes (cut into quarters)
+ 2 cups mixed lettuce (tear lettuce into bite sized pieces)
+ 1 medium orange peeled and sectioned (retain 2 slices with peel for garnish) retain juice from cutting
+ 1/3 cup white vinegar
+ 2 Tbs juice from cutting orange
+ 2 Tbs sugar or honey

Directions:

Place the top 4 ingredients into a salad bowl and toss to combine. In a small mixing bowl combine vinegar, orange juice and sugar and stir until sugar is dissolved. Pour dressing over salad and toss to coat. Serve immediately or chill for 15 minutes.

Cobb Salad

Yields: 2 servings

$3.68

✦1 small head of bib lettuce or ½ head of romaine lettuce (torn into bite-sized pieces)
✦2 slices cooked bacon (crumbled)
✦1 oz cheddar cheese (shredded)
✦1 hardboiled egg (sliced)
✦6 cherry tomatoes (quartered)
✦Ranch dressing (see our recipe under Seasonings, Marinades and Dressings)

Directions:

Place the lettuce, egg, and tomatoes into a salad bowl. Prepare ranch dressing per recipe. (The dressing is best if prepared the night before.) Pour dressing over salad and toss to coat. Add shredded cheddar cheese, sprinkle bacon on top, add cherry tomatoes and sliced hard-boiled egg. Serve immediately or chill for 15 minutes.

Tomato Caprese

Yields: 2 servings

$2.12

- 1 large ripe tomato (sliced in 1/4" pieces)
- ¼ lb mozzarella cheese (fresh queso will work also)
- 6 to 8 fresh basil leaves
- 3 Tbs balsamic vinegar

Directions:

Arrange tomatoes on a serving plate add a slice of cheese or shredded cheese to each tomato and top with torn basil leaves. Drizzle with balsamic vinegar and chill for 30 minutes. This can be served as an appetizer or a side dish. You can also put them on a baking pan and melt the cheese to make a great warm side dish.

Kale and Tomato Salad with Blue Cheese

Yields: 2 servings

$2.84

- 2 – 3 leaves of kale (stemmed and torn into bite sized pieces)
- 1 medium tomato (chopped into 1/2" pieces)
- 1 slice cooked bacon (crumbled)
- 1 oz crumbled blue cheese
- 1 oz balsamic vinegar
- 1 oz extra virgin olive oil

Directions:

Add kale to two salad bowls, top with tomatoes, bacon and blue cheese crumbles. Lightly dress each salad with balsamic vinegar and olive oil. Italian dressing makes a decent substitute for the balsamic and olive oil.

Potatoes, Rice, Pasta, & Yucca

Mojo Yucca

Yields: 6 servings

$1.50

✦ 1 lbs yucca (cassava) peeled and chopped into 2" pieces
✦ 4 to 6 oz of Mojo marinade (see recipe)

Directions:

Peel yucca root and cut into 2" lengths then cut in half lengthwise. Boil yucca for 30 to 45 minutes until tender but not soft. Drain and let cool. Once cool, dice yucca into ½" pieces and place into a resealable plastic bag, then pour in marinade. Refrigerate for up to 24 hours. I like to let the yucca marinate for at least an hour prior to serving. When ready to serve, pour entire contents of bag into a skillet. Cook over medium-low heat until thoroughly warmed. Serve as a tasty side dish in place of potatoes or rice.

Yucca Hash

Recipe Courtesy of Shannon Enete
Yields: 4 servings

$2.32

- 1 yucca
- 1 yellow sweet onion
- 3-4 cloves garlic
- 1 chile dulce pepper
- 1 Tbs butter
- 1 Tbs vegetable / corn oil
- 1 Tsp complete seasoning (green cap)

Cassava and yucca are the same root in the potato family. Its consistency is a bit drier and more fibrous than potatoes earning it a lower glycemic rating. Ticos often use yucca in soup, or boil it and serve as a side. It has a great shelf life when it's not peeled. Because of this, I try to only peel the amount that I plan on cooking. Ok, let's make some hash!

Directions:

Select a small to medium size yucca without any signs of fungal growth. Peel the brown and pink away. Use a sturdy grater or a processor and coarsely grate. Finely dice the onion, garlic, and pepper. In a large bowl mix ingredients. Place the butter and oil in a large nonstick skillet on high. After the oil is warm, spread the ingredients in the pan. Let it pop and sizzle for about 5-7 minutes (varies depending on heat and pan). Turn the heat down to med-high. Peek at the hash with a spatula before you flip, it should be golden brown bordering on dark brown when ready to flip. The second side takes less time. Add oil or butter as needed. Add complete seasoning, salt, and pepper to taste.

* Add roasted garlic and pepper

Potato Salad

Yields: 4 servings

$2.88

- 6 - 7 medium potatoes (skin on, sliced into 1/2" pieces)
- 2 hardboiled eggs
- ½ cup mayonnaise
- 2 Tbs white or cider vinegar
- 1 Tbs yellow mustard
- ¼ cup onion chopped
- 1 celery stalk chopped including leaves
- 2 Tbs dill pickle chopped (optional, pickles are somewhat hard to find)
- salt & pepper to taste

Directions:

Place pieces of potato into a pot with a lid. Fill with water 1" above potatoes. Cook on medium-high heat until potatoes are tender but not mushy. Remove from stove, drain and set aside to cool. Meanwhile mash egg yolks in a small bowl and add mayonnaise, mustard and onion, stir to blend. When potatoes are cooled toss with vinegar to coat. Chop egg whites and toss with potatoes and celery. Add mayonnaise mixture and gentle mix to coat potatoes. Garnish with chopped celery leaves.

French Fries and Yucca Fries

Yields: 2 to 4 servings

$2.44

✦ 2 large potatoes (washed skin on or 1 medium yucca root)
✦ 2 cups vegetable oil
✦ salt as needed

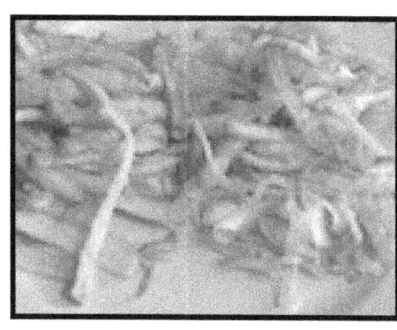

Directions:

Using your Health Craft CR kitchen machine, attach cone number 3 "French fry cone", remove the guard and cut potatoes into French fries. Otherwise, chop potatoes into long thin slices. For yucca, peel and remove both outside rind and pink layer just underneath, proceed with cutting fries.

Heat oil in a large pot or deep-fryer to 350°, and cook fries in batches. Be careful not to overcrowd pot as this will cool the oil too much and cause greasy fries. Fry until potatoes are golden brown or yucca is lightly browned about 6 to 8 minutes per batch. Remove to paper towels and add salt to taste.

* Note: The yucca fries will be crispier than potato fries. They have an excellent taste and will even store for a day and stay crispy. Yucca will not brown as much as potatoes unless overcooked!

Costa Rican Rice

Yields: 4 servings

$1.36

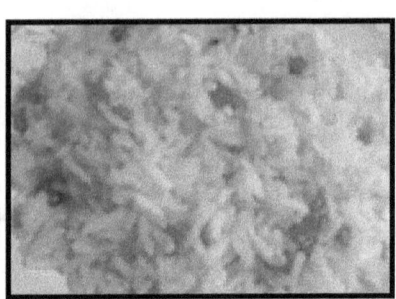

- 1 cup white long grain rice
- 2 Tbs butter or oil
- ½ cup white or yellow onion, diced
- ½ cup red bell pepper, diced
- 1 clove garlic, minced
- 2 cups chicken broth (substitute water if necessary)
- salt and pepper to taste

Directions:

Rinse rice until water runs clear, then drain. Heat butter in a skillet with a cover over medium-high heat. Add rice and stir until rice is slightly browned. Add onions, peppers and garlic and sauté another 2 minutes. Pour in chicken stock and salt and bring to a boil. Stir and reduce heat to medium-low, cover and simmer for 16 minutes. Don't PEEK! After 16 minutes turn off heat and let rice rest for 10 minutes covered. Fluff with fork before serving.

Gallo Pinto

Yields: 4 servings

$1.96

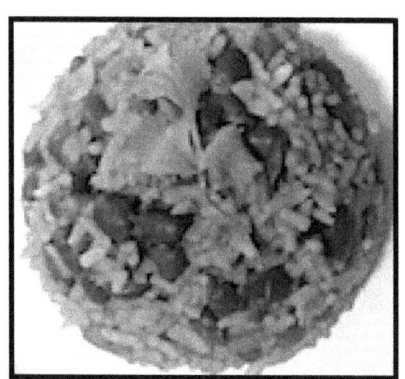

✦Prepare Costa Rican Rice per previous recipe and set aside.
✦1 lbs black or red beans
✦2 Tbs butter or oil
✦1/4 cup white or yellow onion, diced
✦1/8 cup red bell pepper, diced
✦1/2 small jalapeño pepper seeded and diced (optional)
✦salt and pepper to taste
✦2 Tbs Lizano Salsa (green cap)
✦1 Tbs complete seasoning (green cap)

Directions:

Black Beans: Cover beans with water and soak overnight. Drain beans and cover with fresh water, add salt, and bring to a boil. Optionally, add green pepper cut into quarters and seeded. Cover and reduce heat to low and simmer 2 to 3 hours or until beans are tender. (You can also add a chicken bouillon for extra flavor)

Gallo Pinto: Add butter or oil to a large skillet, add onion and red pepper and sauté for two minutes. Add Costa Rican rice (day old rice works best), black beans with a bit of black water, Lizano, complete seasoning, and cilantro. Cook for two to three minutes. Serve with queso fritto, eggs, or by itself. Gallo Pinto is a staple for breakfast and casados.

Once rice and beans are prepared, you can refrigerate or freeze them and prepare smaller batches of Gallo Pinto anytime. Make sure you save black water with the beans, this is what gives extra flavor and color to the Gallo Pinto.

Vegetables

Roasted Cauliflower with Lime Sauce

Yields: 4 servings

$2.48

- ✦1 medium head cauliflower (remove leaves and core)
- ✦2 Tbs vegetable oil
- ✦2 Tbs fresh lime juice
- ✦1 tsp dried oregano
- ✦1 tsp dried basil
- ✦1 tsp dried thyme
- ✦½ tsp onion powder
- ✦2 cloves garlic mashed
- ✦1 tsp fresh ginger smashed
- ✦salt & pepper to taste

Directions:

Prepare marinade by adding all ingredients except cauliflower to a mixing bowl and whisk to combine. Using a basting brush liberally brush all of the marinade onto your cauliflower. Place the head on a baking pan and cook for 45 minutes. Check doneness with a skewer through the head. If not done, return to oven for 15 more minutes. Once the cauliflower is fully cooked, turn the oven to broil and brown the cauliflower. Be careful, keep a watchful eye on it because it will only a few brief moments to brown. Remove and let rest several minutes before serving.

*Optional: Using the same measurements, prepare marinade again and heat on medium in a sauce pan for 3 to 4 minutes. Serve cauliflower with extra marinade on the side.

TIP

The reason we use vegetable oil in this recipe instead of olive oil is because of the cooking temperature. According to studies, olive oil heated at high temperatures (above 350°) begins to burn and can become toxic.

Roasted Broccoli with Balsamic Vinegar

Yields: 4 servings

$2.12

- ✦1 medium head broccoli
- ✦¼ cup olive oil
- ✦3 cloves of garlic minced
- ✦Salt & pepper to taste

Directions:

Pre-heat oven to 350°. Cut the flowerets from the broccoli core. In a large bowl add olive oil, garlic, salt and pepper and whisk to mix. Add broccoli into bowl and toss to thoroughly coat. Spread broccoli on a flat baking pan and roast for 20 to 30 minutes or until tender. Remove to a serving bowl and drizzle with balsamic vinegar to taste.

Coleslaw

Yields: 6 servings

$2.52

- ½ medium head white cabbage
- ½ medium head red cabbage
- 1 medium carrot
- ¾ cup mayonnaise
- 2 Tbs sour cream (natilla)
- 2 Tbs grated onion
- 2 Tbs sugar
- 2 Tbs white vinegar
- 1 Tbs dry mustard (substitute 1 tsp of yellow mustard)
- 2 tsp celery seed
- 1 tsp salt
- 1 tsp black pepper

Directions:

Cut the cabbage into thin strips, or use cone number 4 on your Health Craft CR kitchen machine. Shred carrot using a box shredder or cone number 1. Toss cabbage and carrot together in a large bowl. Mix remaining ingredients in a small bowl until thoroughly combined. Pour dressing over slaw and mix thoroughly. Chill for one hour. Dressing can be made the day before and refrigerated overnight for flavors to meld.

Caramelized Carrots

Yields: 4 servings

$1.00

- ✦2 large carrots washed
- ✦2 Tbs butter plus 2 Tbs
- ✦2 Tbs brown sugar
- ✦salt & pepper to taste

Directions:

Wash carrots but do not peel, most vegetables have their vitamins and minerals in the skin or just under the skin. Slice carrots as uniformly as possible, this allows for even cooking. Add 2 Tbs of butter to skillet and sauté carrots over medium low heat until soft but al dente. When carrots are done, add 2 more Tbs of butter to skillet and melt. Increase heat to medium-high, sprinkle brown sugar over carrots, and sauté stirring constantly until all carrots are coated and sugar is melted. Remove from heat and let rest 2 minutes then serve.

Wilted Kale and Tomato with Parmesan Reggiano

Yields: 2 servings

$2.60

- 1 large bunch of kale (washed & stemmed)
- 2 Tbs butter or olive oil
- 1 clove garlic minced
- 5 – 6 cherry tomatoes or a small tomato diced and seeded
- 2 Tbs parmesan reggiano (substitute blue cheese or goat cheese)
- salt & pepper to taste

Directions:

In a skillet with a lid, add butter or olive oil and heat over medium heat. Add garlic and sauté 2 minutes then add kale and tomatoes and toss while sautéing to coat. Cook 3 to 4 minutes or until kale is wilted. Add salt and pepper to taste. Remove to a serving platter and grate parmesan reggiano on top. Serve immediately.

Fried Sweet Plantains

Yields: 2 servings

$1.02

In Costa Rica and many Latin countries, plantains are served with almost every meal. Cooking the plantain takes a little practice to get it right. There are two main ways to cook plantains, green and ripe! Green plantains are usually pressed to form a flat circle before frying and are not sweet at all but more savory. A ripe plantain should be almost black. When it looks like you should throw it out, it's ready to cook!

- 1 large ripe plantain
- 2 Tbs butter
- 1 Tbs of brown sugar

Directions:

Peel ripe plantain and slice about 1" thick and slightly on the bias. Heat a skillet over medium heat and add butter. When butter stops foaming add plantains but do not crowd the skillet. In an eleven inch skillet you should be able to cook one whole plantain. Cook for 2 to 3 minutes per side. When done sprinkle with brown sugar, cover and cook for additional 2 minutes. Plantains will be soft and sweet.

Grilled Plantains

Recipe courtesy of *Shannon Enete*
Yields: 3 servings

$0.35

✦Ripe plantain (see Produce 101)

Directions:

Lay your plantain on a cutting board and slice off the ends, leaving a bit of yellow plantain exposed on each end. Place on a grill with medium-high heat. Grill until the peel is black and beginning to bubble, then turn over. When both sides of the peel are bubbly and the plantain innards begin to ooze out, your plantain is ready to eat. Remove from the grill and delicately slice down the peel. Fold the peel back, cslice and serve as a sweet side.

TIP
If you don't have a grill, or the time, take a ripe plantain and slice a slit down the length of the fruit, then place in the microwave on high heat for 3 minutes. The taste is almost exactly the same as the grilled plantain!

Desserts

Peach Cobbler

Yields: 4 servings

$4.04

- ¼ cup butter
- ½ cup all-purpose flour
- ½ cup white sugar
- ½ cup light brown sugar
- 1 ½ tsp baking powder
- pinch of salt
- ½ cup milk
- 2-3 medium ripe peaches
- dash of cinnamon or nutmeg

Directions:

Pre-heat oven to 375°. Pour melted butter into a 9" pie pan. In a mixing bowl combine flour, ¼ cup of each sugar, baking powder and salt, mix well. Stir in milk, do not over mix, stir until just combined. Pour batter over butter and don't mix!

In a saucepan combine peaches, lemon juice, and remaining sugar. Bring to a boil over high heat, stirring constantly. Cook until peaches are softened and sugar is melted, about 5 to 6 minutes. Spoon peaches over batter, do not stir, make sure you spread the peaches to cover the entire pan. Sprinkle with cinnamon or nutmeg. Bake for 35 to 45 minutes or until top is nicely browned. Serve warm or cold.

Apple Crisp

Yields: 4 – 6 servings

$3.80

Filling:
- 2 Tbs butter
- ¼ cup brown sugar
- 5 – 6 medium baking apples

Topping:
- 1 cup brown sugar
- ½ cup flour
- 1 cup quick oats
- ½ tsp cinnamon
- ½ tsp salt
- 3 to 4 Tbs butter
- 1 tsp vanilla extract

Directions:

Pre-heat oven to 350°.

For Filling: Peel and core apples and slice into ¼ inch wedges. Melt 2 Tbs of butter in a saucepan over medium heat, then stir in ¼ cup brown sugar. Cook until sugar is dissolved, then add apples. Stir to coat the apples with the sugar mixture and cook until apples are slightly softened. Pour cooked apples into a 9" greased pie pan.

For Topping: Combine all dry ingredients in a mixing bowl. Melt butter and stir in vanilla extract. Pour butter and vanilla into the dry ingredients slowly, mixing by hand just until moistened. Mixture should be clumpy, resembling granola. Pour topping over apple mixture and spread out evenly. Bake at 350° for 30 to 45 minutes or until topping is nicely browned and apples are bubbly. Allow to cool for ten minutes before cutting and serve warm, cold, or a la mode.

Arroz con Leche
(Rice Pudding)
Yields: 6 to 8 servings
$4.48

- 1 cup long grain rice
- 2 cups water
- 2 cups milk
- ½ cup sugar
- 1 can evaporated milk
- 1 can sweetened condensed milk
- ½ cup raisins
- 1 Tbs vanilla extract
- 1 tsp cinnamon
- ½ tsp nutmeg
- Dash of cinnamon

Directions:

After scouring the internet and researching rice pudding, we found dozens of variations! All Latin American countries have their own little twists. The recipe above is our version of a true Costa Rican Rice Pudding.

In a 4 quart stock pot bring water to a boil, add rice, stir, reduce heat to low and cover. Cook rice 16 minutes, do not peek, remove lid and fluff with a fork. While rice is cooking, in a large mixing bowl whisk condensed milk, evaporated milk, vanilla, sugar, cinnamon and nutmeg together until well blended. When rice is done cooking, slowly stir in 2 cups milk and simmer over low heat for 10 minutes, stirring continuously. Add milk mixture, raisins and cook, stirring constantly for an addition 10 to 15 minutes or until desired thickness is achieved. Remember pudding will thicken more as it cools! Serve at room temperature or chilled. Sprinkle a dash of cinnamon on top and serve.

** If you prefer your pudding "white," omit cinnamon and nutmeg in the milk mixture. Use both a dash of cinnamon and nutmeg on top when serving.

Tres Leches Cake

Yields: 6 – 8 servings

$5.18

Cake:
- 4 eggs separated
- 2 cups all-purpose flour
- 1 cup sugar
- 1 tsp baking powder
- 2 Tbs water

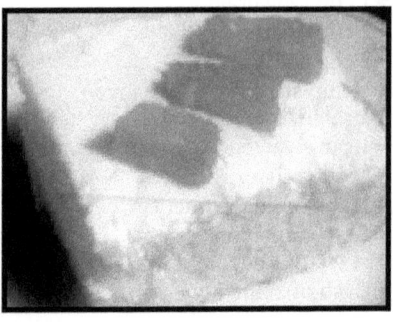

Filling:
- 1 can (10 oz) sweetened condensed milk
- 1 can evaporated milk (8 oz)
- 1 cup whole milk

Topping:
- 1 cup heavy whipping cream
- 2 – 3 Tbs sugar

Directions:

Pre-heat oven to 325°

For Cake: Separate the egg whites and yolks. In a small bowl add flour, sugar, and baking powder and thoroughly mix. Set aside. In a large mixing bowl add egg whites and beat until fluffy and stiff. Add egg yolks one at a time and continue to mix. Add flour mixture a little at a time and mix until well blended. Add water and blend. Pour batter into a 9" x 13" greased baking dish. Bake at 325° for 25 to 30 minutes (times may vary depending on your oven). After 25 minutes check cake with a toothpick, if it comes out clean it is done. Remove from oven and use a fork to make uniform holes over the entire cake, being careful not to tear up the top.

For Filling: Mix together "Tres Leches", the three milks, whisk until well combined. Pour milk mixture slowly over the entire cake as uniformly as possible and allow to soak in before adding more.

For Topping: Add 1 cup of whipping cream to a mixing bowl. Mix on high speed until fluffy and has peaks. Slowly add sugar and continue to mix until all sugar is blended. Do not over mix or topping will break! Spoon whipped cream over the entire cake. Refrigerate until ready to serve.

You may garnish the cake when serving with your favorite fresh fruits.

Sautéed Pineapple with Rum

Yields: 4 servings

$2.04

This recipe requires a "Flambé." Caution should be taken in preparation

- 2 cups fresh pineapple peeled, cored and sliced
- ½ cup Captain Morgan Spiced Rum
- ½ cup light brown sugar
- 2 Tbs butter

While traveling around Costa Rica when we first arrived ,we came upon a quaint little restaurant in La Fortuna called Novillito's Steak House. We had the sautéed pineapple there. We had never tried anything like it. We asked the chef how it was made and of course the next chance we got, we had to attempt to recreate it. We made it for all the kids we met at a hostel in Monteverde and they loved it.

Directions:

Peel and core pineapple and cut into bite sized pieces. In a skillet melt 2 tablespoons of butter over medium heat and sauté for 5 minutes or so. Add brown sugar and stir constantly until melted and pineapple is coated. Add rum to pan and ignite with a long tipped lighter. Stir pineapple to cook off alcohol. If cooking on a gas stove, remove skillet for stove before adding rum. Remove and serve in bowls; serve warm.

Happy Hour Cocktails

Pina Colada

Yields: 2 drinks

$3.48

- 4 oz fresh pineapple cubed
- ½ cup coconut cream
- ¼ cup coconut milk
- 4 oz white rum
- 1 Tbs sugar
- 1 ½ cups ice
- pineapple wedge for garnish

Directions:

    Combine all ingredients in a blender and puree until smooth. Pour into tall glass and garnish with pineapple wedge.

Frozen Mango Margarita

Yields: 2 drinks

$2.30

- 10 oz fresh mango (about ½ a large mango)
- 1 fresh lime juice and zest
- 1 Tbs coarse salt
- 3 oz of tequila
- 3 oz triple sec
- 1 Tbs sugar
- 1 ½ cups ice
- mango wedge for garnish

Directions:

Combine all ingredients in a blender and puree until smooth. Place 2 Tbs of coarse salt on a flat dish add lime zest and combine, rub rim of margarita glass with lime wedge, roll rim in lime salt. Pour margarita into glass and garnish.

Frozen Strawberry Daiquiri

Yields: 2 drinks

$2.02

- 1 ½ cups ice
- 4 Tbs white sugar
- 6 to 8 fresh strawberries stemmed
- 2 tsp fresh lime juice
- 2 Tbs fresh squeezed lemon juice
- 3 ounces of good rum
- lime or lemon wedge for garnish

Directions:

Combine all ingredients in a blender (only 2 Tbs sugar) and puree until smooth. Place remaining 2 Tbs of sugar on a flat dish, rub rim of daiquiri glass with lime wedge, roll rim in sugar. Pour daiquiri into glass and garnish.

Cacique Guaro Sour

Yields: 1 drink

$1.29

✦2 ounces of Cacique Guaro
✦2 ounces fresh squeezed lemon juice

✳Optional- add 1 ounce of Kola syrup

Directions:

Pour ingredients into mixing glass, stir to combine, pour over ice and garnish with lemon wedge.

Cucumber/Basil Mojito

Yields: 1 drink

$1.74

- 3 - 1/8" slices of cucumber
- 6 to 8 basil leaves
- 2 lime slices
- 3 ounces good rum
- 2 tsp sugar
- 2 ounces club soda
- 1 cucumber slice for garnish
- 1 basil sprig for garnish

Directions:

Put cucumbers, basil, lime slices, rum, and sugar in a cocktail shaker. Muddle (crush) ingredients together until sugar is dissolved. Add some ice, cover and shake vigorously. Strain into chilled glass filled with ice. Add club soda and garnish.

www.ingramcontent.com/pod-product-compliance
Lightning Source LLC
Chambersburg PA
CBHW061327040426
42444CB00011B/2806